Las Vegas ACES

by Luke Hanlon

Copyright © 2026 by Press Room Editions. All rights reserved. No part of this book may be used or reproduced in any manner whatsoever, including internet usage, without written permission from the copyright owner, except in the case of brief quotations embodied in critical articles and reviews.

Book design by Kate Liestman
Cover design by Kate Liestman

Photographs ©: M. Anthony Nesmith/Icon Sportswire/AP Images, cover; Sarah Stier/Getty Images Sport/Getty Images, 4, 9; Frank Franklin II/AP Images, 7; Todd Warshaw/Getty Images Sport/Getty Images, 10; Jason Wise/AP Images, 13; Otto Greule Jr./Allsport/Getty Images Sport/Getty Images, 15; Christian Petersen/Getty Images Sport/Getty Images, 16, 25; Roy Dabner/AP Images, 18; Pat Lovell/Cal Sports Media/AP Images, 21; Leon Bennett/Getty Images Sport/Getty Images, 22; Maddie Meyer/Getty Images Sport/Getty Images, 27; Candice Ward/Getty Images Sport/Getty Images, 29

Press Box Books, an imprint of Press Room Editions.

ISBN
979-8-89469-014-8 (library bound)
979-8-89469-027-8 (paperback)
979-8-89469-052-0 (epub)
979-8-89469-040-7 (hosted ebook)

Library of Congress Control Number: 2025930750

Distributed by North Star Editions, Inc.
2297 Waters Drive
Mendota Heights, MN 55120
www.northstareditions.com

Printed in the United States of America
082025

ABOUT THE AUTHOR

Luke Hanlon is a sportswriter and editor based in Minneapolis. He's written dozens of nonfiction sports books for kids and spends a lot of his free time watching his favorite Minnesota sports teams.

TABLE of CONTENTS

CHAPTER 1
BACK TO BACK   **5**

CHAPTER 2
SHOOTING STARZZ   **11**

CHAPTER 3
ADDING STARS   **17**

CHAPTER 4
COMING UP ACES   **23**

SUPERSTAR PROFILE
A'JA WILSON   **28**

QUICK STATS	**30**
GLOSSARY	**31**
TO LEARN MORE	**32**
INDEX	**32**

CHAPTER 1

BACK TO BACK

A'ja Wilson received a pass. The Las Vegas Aces center dribbled the ball with her back to the hoop. New York Liberty center Jonquel Jones guarded her closely. With the shot clock winding down, Wilson needed to make a move. She picked up her dribble and turned around. Wilson rose up for a shot. Jones put

A'ja Wilson averaged 21.3 points per game in the 2023 Finals.

her hand right in Wilson's face. But the ball still fell through the net.

The Aces were playing in the 2023 Women's National Basketball Association (WNBA) Finals. They were looking to make history. No team had won two straight titles in 21 years. Las Vegas entered Game 4 with a chance to win the series in New York. Wilson's jump shot put the Aces up 70–64 with 1:26 left in the game. Another championship was within reach.

The Liberty refused to go down easily, though. On the next possession, New York guard Courtney Vandersloot hit a three-pointer. Then she stole the ball from Aces guard Kelsey Plum. The Liberty

Wilson (22) drives to the basket during Game 4 of the 2023 Finals.

scored two points off the turnover. Suddenly, the Aces led by only one.

Las Vegas failed to score on the next possession. The Liberty now had 17 seconds to extend the series. They got the ball to Breanna Stewart, the league's

RESILIENT TEAM

Many Las Vegas players suffered injuries in 2023. That included All-Star guard Chelsea Gray. In Game 3 of the Finals, Gray left with a foot injury. The Aces had to play Game 4 without their team's assist leader. But they overcame Gray's injury to win the title.

Most Valuable Player (MVP). But Aces forward Alysha Clark played tight defense. She forced Stewart to give up the ball. Time was running out for New York.

With 2.4 seconds left, Vandersloot received the ball in the corner. Aces guard Jackie Young flew toward her to guard the shot. The ball never hit the rim. The buzzer sounded before the Liberty could shoot again.

Wilson raised her hands into the air. The Aces players all ran to midcourt.

The Aces celebrate winning the 2023 Finals.

They mobbed one another in celebration. For the second straight year, the Aces were champions!

CHAPTER 2

SHOOTING STARZZ

The history of the Las Vegas Aces started in Salt Lake City, Utah. The WNBA held its first season in 1997. The Utah Starzz were one of the league's original eight teams.

The Starzz struggled in their first two seasons. In 1997 and 1998, they won 15 out of 58 games. All those losses helped Utah receive high

Margo Dydek (12) averaged 12.9 points per game in 1998.

draft picks. In 1998, the Starzz had the top pick in the draft. They used it on towering center Margo Dydek. At 7-foot-2 (218-cm), Dydek was the tallest player in the WNBA. She used her height to easily block shots.

In 1999, Utah needed a scorer. The Starzz found one in Natalie Williams. Utah drafted the center with the third pick that year. Williams had been playing in a different league. So, she entered the WNBA as a 28-year-old rookie. Her experience showed right away. Williams averaged 18 points per game in 1999.

In 2000, Williams and Dydek lifted Utah to its first winning record. A year later, the duo led the Starzz into the playoffs for

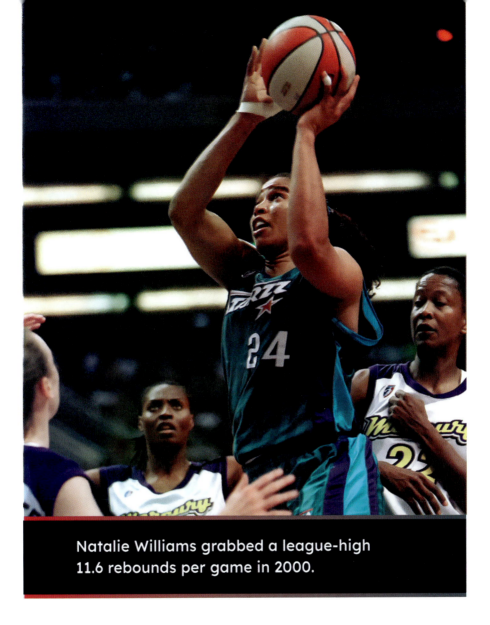

Natalie Williams grabbed a league-high 11.6 rebounds per game in 2000.

the first time. However, the Sacramento Monarchs swept them in the first round.

The Starzz came back stronger in 2002. Veteran forward Adrienne Goodson put

HISTORIC PERFORMANCE

On June 7, 2001, Margo Dydek put on a show. The center blocked 10 shots against the Orlando Miracle. She became the first WNBA player to tally 10 blocks in a game. Dydek also scored 12 points and grabbed 11 rebounds. That marked the second triple-double in league history.

together an All-Star season. So did young guard Marie Ferdinand-Harris. The Starzz faced the Houston Comets in the playoffs. The teams split the first two games in the series. Houston hosted a decisive Game 3. Williams scored 25 points to lead the Starzz to their first playoff series win.

The Starzz lost to the Los Angeles Sparks in the semifinals. That series ended up being the final games for the

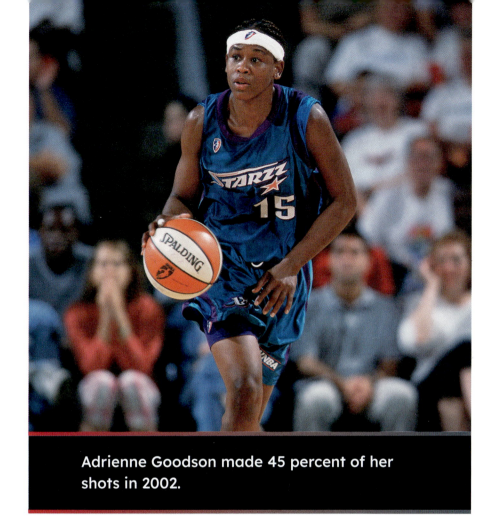

Adrienne Goodson made 45 percent of her shots in 2002.

Utah Starzz. After the season, the team moved to Texas and became the San Antonio Silver Stars. The team suffered three straight losing seasons in its new city. However, the bad times would soon be over.

CHAPTER 3

ADDING STARS

In the 2006 draft, the Silver Stars took Sophia Young-Malcolm with the fourth pick. The forward led San Antonio in scoring as a rookie. But the team still finished with a losing record.

Before the 2007 season, the Silver Stars made a big move. They traded two first-round picks to the New York Liberty. In return, San Antonio

Sophia Young-Malcolm scored 12 points per game as a rookie.

Becky Hammon averaged a league-high five assists per game in 2007.

received Becky Hammon. The All-Star guard turned the Silver Stars around. Hammon led the team to its first playoff berth in five years.

San Antonio faced the Sacramento Monarchs in the first round. In a decisive Game 3, the score was tied 78–78. Hammon had the ball in the game's final seconds. She drove hard into the paint. Then she bounced a pass to Vickie Johnson. The guard scored from close range to send San Antonio to the semifinals.

The Phoenix Mercury ended San Antonio's run. But the Silver Stars built on their success. In 2008, they finished with the league's best record. The Silver Stars then beat the Monarchs in the first round. The semifinals came down to a Game 3 against the Los Angeles Sparks. San Antonio trailed 72–69 with just over a minute to play. Hammon then scored the game's final seven points. Her heroics sent the Silver Stars to the WNBA Finals.

The dream run came to a quick end for San Antonio. The Detroit Shock swept the series. Even so, the Silver Stars looked ready to compete for years. They made the playoffs in each of the next four seasons. But each time, they lost in the first round.

Hammon and Young-Malcolm both missed the 2013 season with

SAN ANTONIO ALL-STARS

San Antonio hosted the 2011 WNBA All-Star Game. Becky Hammon played in the game. But that wasn't her only honor of the day. The WNBA celebrated its 15th anniversary by naming the 15 best players in league history. Hammon made the list.

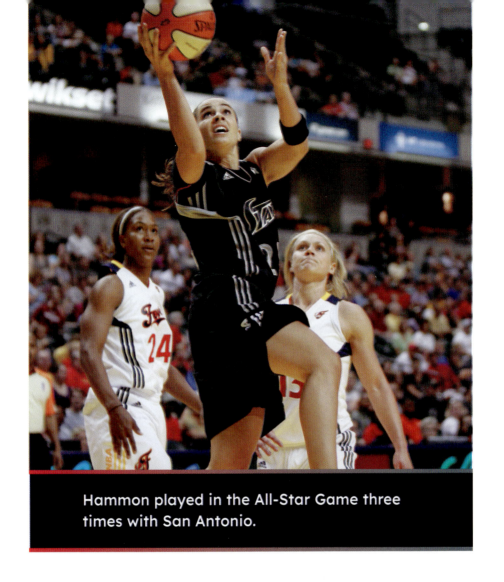

Hammon played in the All-Star Game three times with San Antonio.

injuries. Without their stars, San Antonio missed the playoffs for the first time in seven years. By 2016, Hammon and Young-Malcolm had retired. The team would soon start a rebuild in a new city.

COMING UP ACES

Losing seasons piled up in San Antonio. So, the team went up for sale in 2017. Before the 2018 season, the team moved to Nevada and became the Las Vegas Aces. The team quickly added talent in the draft.

Kelsey Plum made the move from San Antonio to Las Vegas. The guard had been the top pick in 2017. With the

Kelsey Plum averaged four assists per game in 2018.

first pick in 2018, the Aces selected A'ja Wilson. A year later, Las Vegas drafted guard Jackie Young with the top pick.

All three players developed into stars. In 2019, the trio led the Aces to the playoffs. In 2020, the team reached the Finals, even without an injured Plum. However, the Seattle Storm swept the series.

Before the 2021 season, the Aces signed All-Star guard Chelsea Gray. The team had an excellent year.

DRAMATIC WIN

In 2019, the Aces played their first playoff game in Las Vegas. Up by two points, the Chicago Sky had the ball in the final seconds. Aces forward Dearica Hamby stole a pass. Then she launched a shot near half-court. The ball fell through the basket, giving Las Vegas the win.

Chelsea Gray (12) played in the All-Star Game in her first season with the Aces.

But Las Vegas lost in the semifinals. After the season, the Aces hired Becky Hammon as their coach.

Under Hammon's guidance, the Aces took off. In 2022, Las Vegas cruised into the semifinals to face Seattle. The Aces

25

had a chance to close out the series in Game 4. With the score tied 87–87, Gray drained two clutch buckets. The win sent Las Vegas back to the Finals.

The Aces proved to be too much for the Connecticut Sun. Young, Plum, Gray, and Wilson all averaged more than 12 points per game. The Aces won the series in four games to clinch their first title.

Las Vegas didn't slow down in 2023. The Aces won a WNBA-record 34 games. Then they won five straight playoff games to return to the Finals. The New York Liberty had signed three All-Stars before the 2023 season. But they still couldn't stop Las Vegas. The Aces won their second straight championship.

Hammon (right) celebrates with Wilson after the Aces won the 2022 Finals.

Hammon led the Aces back to the semifinals in 2024. However, they fell to the Liberty. Even so, the Aces remained loaded with stars. Fans hoped it wouldn't be long before Las Vegas won another title.

SUPERSTAR PROFILE

A'JA WILSON

A'ja Wilson wasted no time becoming one of the best players in the WNBA. In 2018, she averaged 20.7 points and 8 rebounds per game. Wilson received every vote for the Rookie of the Year Award. That honor would prove to be the first of many in her career.

At 6-foot-4 (193-cm), Wilson could score easily in the post. On defense, she swatted away shots close to the basket, making it tough for opponents to score. In 2023, Wilson won her second straight Defensive Player of the Year Award.

In 2024, Wilson put together one of the greatest seasons in WNBA history. She scored 1,021 points. That broke the WNBA record for most points in a season. Wilson also grabbed a league-record 451 rebounds. Those records helped Wilson win the MVP Award for the third time in her career.

Wilson (22) averaged a career-high 2.6 blocks per game in 2024.

QUICK STATS

LAS VEGAS ACES

Team history: Utah Starzz (1997–2002), San Antonio Silver Stars (2003–13), San Antonio Stars (2014–17), Las Vegas Aces (2018–)

Championships: 2 (2022, 2023)

Key coaches:
- Dan Hughes (2005–09, 2011–16): 161–213, 8–16 playoffs
- Bill Laimbeer (2018–21): 77–45, 7–11 playoffs
- Becky Hammon (2022–): 87–29, 19–6 playoffs, 2 WNBA titles

Most career points: A'ja Wilson (4,782)

Most career assists: Becky Hammon (1,133)

Most career rebounds: A'ja Wilson (2,087)

Most career blocks: Margo Dydek (655)

Most career steals: Sophia Young-Malcolm (477)

Stats are accurate through the 2024 season.

GLOSSARY

clutch
Having to do with a difficult situation when the outcome of the game is in question.

draft
An event that allows teams to choose new players coming into the league.

paint
The area between the basket and the free-throw line.

post
The area near the basket where centers often play.

rookie
A first-year player.

swept
Won all the games in a series.

triple-double
When a player reaches 10 or more of three different statistics in one game.

turnover
When a player loses the ball to the other team.

TO LEARN MORE

O'Neal, Ciara. *The WNBA Finals*. Apex Editions, 2023.

Tischler, Joe. *A'ja Wilson*. Amicus Learning, 2025.

Whiting, Jim. *The Story of the Las Vegas Aces*. Creative Education, 2024.

MORE INFORMATION

To learn more about the Las Vegas Aces, go to **pressboxbooks.com/AllAccess**. These links are routinely monitored and updated to provide the most current information available.

INDEX

Chicago Sky, 24
Clark, Alysha, 8
Connecticut Sun, 26

Detroit Shock, 20
Dydek, Margo, 12, 14

Ferdinand-Harris, Marie, 14

Goodson, Adrienne, 13
Gray, Chelsea, 8, 24, 26

Hamby, Dearica, 24
Hammon, Becky, 18–21, 25, 27
Houston Comets, 14

Johnson, Vickie, 19
Jones, Jonquel, 5–6

Los Angeles Sparks, 14, 19

New York Liberty, 5–8, 17, 26–27

Orlando Miracle, 14

Phoenix Mercury, 19
Plum, Kelsey, 6, 23–24, 26

Sacramento Monarchs, 13, 19
Seattle Storm, 24–25
Stewart, Breanna, 7–8

Vandersloot, Courtney, 6, 8

Williams, Natalie, 12, 14
Wilson, A'ja, 5–6, 8, 24, 26, 28

Young, Jackie, 8, 24, 26
Young-Malcolm, Sophia, 17, 20–21